ALGEBRA FUNDAMENTALS

WORKBOOK

Acknowledgements

The author and publisher are grateful to the copyright holders for permission to use quoted materials and images.

Published by Inspire Studies.

ISBN 9798435177831

First published in 2022

Author: Teresa Maine
Editor: Gordon Goulding, Kavitha Sree
Cover Design: Roman Derkach
Proof reading by Proofed.

Contents

1. Using Algebraic Expressions

Example:

Grace buys 15 cakes. The price of each cake is £W. How much does Grace have to pay in total?

Solution:

The price of each cake is £W, and in total, she buys 15 pieces of cake.

$$£W \times 15 = £15W$$

Hence, Grace has to pay £W times 15 pieces, which equals £$15W$.

Example:

There are P red balls in a box, and Joe puts 5 more red balls in the box. How many red balls does Joe have altogether?

Solution:

The number of red balls was P initially, and then Joe added five more red balls. Therefore, the total number of red balls is $P + 5$.

Exercise 1:

1. Susan earns £850 monthly. She spends £a on travel, £b on food and £c on rent. She saves the rest of the money. How much has she saved after three months?

_____

2. A shop sells K bottles of milk every week. How many bottles will the shop sell after six weeks?

_____

3. Four boxes of chocolates cost £Q. What is the cost of one box of chocolate?

_____

4. A school has S number of girls and T number of boys. What is the total number of students in the school?

_____

5. The price of each apple is £0.5, and each banana costs £0.35. John bought R number of apples and Q number of bananas. How much will John have to pay?

_____

2. Simplifying Expressions by Collecting Like Terms

Example:

$a + 3a + 5b + 2b + 4 + 5$

Solution:

$a + 3a = 4a$ Add the expressions with like terms.

$5b + 2b = 7b$

$4 + 5 = 9$

$a + 3a + 5b + 2b + 4 + 5$

$= 4a + 7b + 9$

Example:

$2x^2 + y^2 - 4y^2 + 4x^2$

Solution:

$2x^2 + 4x^2 = 6x^2$ Add the expressions with like terms.

$y^2 - 4y^2 = -3y^2$

$2x^2 + y^2 - 4y^2 + 4x^2$

$= 6x^2 - 3y^2$

Exercise 2:

1.   Fully simplify these expressions:

(a) $5t + 8t$

_____

(b) $3b + 4b - b$

_____

(c) $6s - 2s + s$

_____

(d) $9n + 2n - n$

_____

(e) $-5m + 2 - 7m + 6$

_____

(f) $12t - 3 + 8 - 3t$

_____

2. Fully simplify these expressions:

(a) $3x + 8y - x - 2y$

_____

(b) $6a + 2a - b + 5b - a$

_____

(c) $3s - 2t + 6s - 5t$

(d) $7p - 3q - 2p - q$

(e) $2m + 8n - 4m - 2n$

(f) $12a - 5b + 6a - 3b$

3. Fully simplify these expressions:

(a) $3x^2 + 6x^2 + 8x^2$

(b) $9y^2 - 2y^2 + 6y^2$

(c) $4a^2 - 2a^2 + 5a^2$

(d) $7b^2 - 4b^2 - 2b^2$

(e) $5n^2 - 6 + 4n^2 - 3$

(f) $11m^2 + m - 2m^2 + 3m + 2$

4. Fully simplify these expressions:

(a) $2ab + ab + 4ab$

(b) $5xy - 2xy + x^2$

(c) $4pq - pq - p^2$

(d) $-3fg + 6f^2g^2 + 5fg - 2f^2g^2$

(e) $3s^2 - 4t^2 + 3s^2 - 2t^2 + 7st - 2st$

(f) $5mn - 5m^2n + 11mn + 12m^2n + 2g - 3g$

5. Write an expression for the perimeter of each shape:

(a) A rectangle

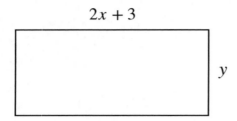

_____

(b) A regular hexagon

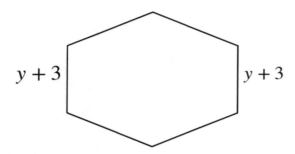

_____

(c) A triangle

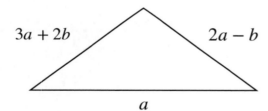

_____

(d) A trapezium

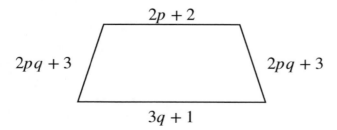

_____

3. Multiplying and Dividing Terms with Powers

Example:

$$5a^2b \times 6ab^2c$$

Solution:

$5 \times 6 = 30$ Multiply the expressions with like terms.

$a^2 \times a = a^3$

$b \times b^2 = b^3$

$c \times 1 = c$

$5a^2b \times 6ab^2c = 30a^3b^3c$

Example:

$$\frac{12a^3b^4c^5}{2ab^2c}$$

Solution:

$12 \div 2 = 6$ Divide the expressions with like terms.

$a^3 \div a = a^2$

$b^4 \div b^2 = b^2$

$c^5 \div c = C^4$

$$\frac{12a^3b^4c^5}{2ab^2c} = 6a^2b^2c^4$$

Exercise 3:

1. Simplify these expressions to their simplest forms:

(a) $-5 \times p \times p$

(b) $4r \times 5r$

(c) $-2q \times -3q$

(d) $6k \times -3k$

(e) $-11t \times 3t \times -t$

(f) $8a \times -4a \times 2a$

2. Simplify these expressions to their simplest forms:

(a) $\dfrac{1}{3}p \times \dfrac{6}{4}q \times p$

(b) $-\dfrac{1}{3}s \times 10 \times -\dfrac{3}{10}t$

(c) $-\dfrac{5}{18}a \times b \times \dfrac{4}{10}a^2$

(d) $-\dfrac{2}{5}g \times g^2 \times \dfrac{5}{6}h^2$

(d) $-\dfrac{1}{5}m \times 3n \times \dfrac{2}{6}n$

(e) $\dfrac{2}{7}g \times 2f \times \dfrac{14}{10} \times 5f$

3. Simplify these expressions to their simplest forms:

(a) $(a^2)^3$

(b) $(k^{-7})^2$

(c) $(4g^3)^{-3}$

(d) $(2m^2n^3)^3$

(e) $3 \times (6s^2t^3)^{-2}$

(f) $(2p^{-3}q^{-2})^3$

4. Simplify these expressions to their simplest forms:

(a) $\dfrac{y^5}{y^3}$

(b) $\dfrac{b^6}{b^3}$

(c) $\dfrac{18k^5}{9k^2}$

(d) $\dfrac{15x^4}{3x^2}$

(e) $\dfrac{26m^5n^3}{13m^2n}$

(f) $\dfrac{28p^6q^4}{7p^2q^2}$

5. Simplify these expressions to their simplest forms:

(a) $\dfrac{9ab^4c^5}{3a^2c^2}$

(b) $\dfrac{45m^6m^4}{5m^2n^2}$

(c) $\dfrac{3st}{4sp} \times \dfrac{8st}{6s^2}$

(d) $\dfrac{2a^3b^2 \times 6a^2b^2}{6a^4b^2}$

(e) $\dfrac{4m^2n^4p^2 \times 3m^3n^2p^3}{6m^2n^4p^2}$

(f) $\dfrac{6ab^2c \times 8a^3bc^5}{2a^2bc^4}$

6. Write the expression for the area of each shape in its simplest form. All lengths are in cm.

(a)

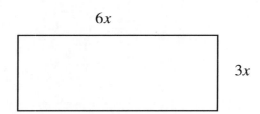

_____

(b)

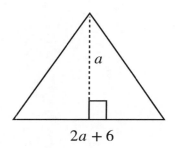

_____

(C)

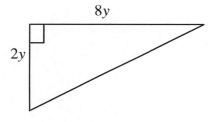

_____

(d)

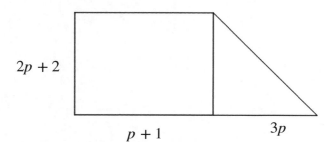

_____

4. Expanding Single or Double Brackets

Example:

$2x(x + 4)$

Solution:

$2x \times x = 2x^2$ Multiply out each term inside the bracket

$2x \times 4 = 8x$ by the term outside the bracket.

$2x(x + 4) = 2x^2 + 8x$

Example:

$3(y + 2) - 4(y - 1)$

Solution:

$3 \times y + 3 \times 2 = 3y + 6$ Multiply out each term inside the bracket

by the term outside the bracket.

$-4 \times y - 4 \times (-1) = -4y - 4$

$3(y + 2) - 4(y - 1)$

$= 3y + 6 - 4y - 4$

$= -y + 10$ Collect like terms

Exercise 4:

1. Expand these expressions:

(a) $4(a + 2)$

(b) $-6(b - 3)$

(c) $-5(m - n)$

(d) $11(x + 2y)$

(e) $9(3p - 4q - 1)$

(f) $-2(-4x^2 + 2x + 3)$

2. Expand these expressions:

(a) $5a(b + 3)$

(b) $3p(q + 2)$

(c) $4b(b + 2c)$

(d) $6m(2m + 5n)$

(e) $8t(4t - 3s)$

(f) $4x(2x - y)$

3. Expand these expressions:

(a) $-3b(2a + 6b)$

(b) $-5g(3a + 2g)$

(c) $-2e(2f - 3g)$

(d) $-3x(5x - 2y)$

(e) $7(x - 2) + 6$

(f) $9(2a + 3) - 5a$

4. Expand and fully simplify these expressions:

(a) $2(a + 1) + 4(5a + 3)$

(b) $6(b + 3) + 2(3b + 5)$

(c) $4(p + 4) + 5(2p - 3)$

(d) $7(2t + 2) + 3(4t - 5)$

(e) $-3(3c + 5) + 2(6c - 4)$

(f) $-6(2m + 7) + 7(3m - 2)$

5. Expand and fully simplify theses expressions:

(a) $3(2d - 3) - 6(4d - 6)$

(b) $7(3p - 2) - 5(3p - 11)$

(c) $6p + 2(3p + 2) + 4(2p + 6)$

(d) $-2a(a - 3) - 5b(b + 3)$

(e) $3k(k - 5) - 2q(q - 2)$

(f) $4m(m - 9) - 3n(n - 5)$

6. Write an expression for each area shown below. All measurements are in cm.

(a)

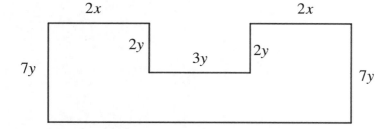

(b)

(c)

(d)

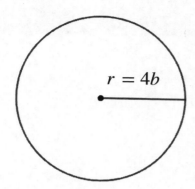

$r = 4b$

(e)

$2m + 3n$

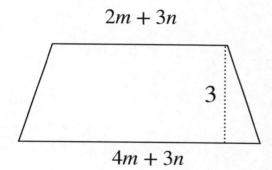

3

$4m + 3n$

5. Expanding Three Brackets

Example:

$(y - 6)(y - 5)(y + 2)$

Solution:

$(y - 6)(y - 5)$ Multiply out each term inside the bracket.

$= y^2 - 5y - 6y + 30 = y^2 - 11y + 30$

$(y^2 - 11y + 30)(y + 2)$

$= y^3 - 11y^2 + 30y + 2y^2 - 22y + 60$

$= y^3 - 9y^2 + 8y + 60$

Example:

$2(x - 3)^3$

Solution:

$2(x - 3)(x - 3)(x - 3)$ Multiply out each term inside the bracket.

$= 2(x^2 - 6x + 9)(x - 3)$

$= 2(x^3 - 6x^2 + 9x - 3x^2 + 18x - 27)$

$= 2(x^3 - 9x^2 + 27x - 27)$

$= 2x^3 - 18x^2 + 54x - 54$

Exercise 5:

1. Fully expand and simplify these expressions:

(a) $(m + 5)(m - 2)(m + 3)$

(b) $(m - 3)(m + 6)(m + 2)$

(c) $(m - 2)(m - 4)(m - 1)$

(d) $(2m - 1)(3m + 2)(4m + 1)$

(e) $(3m - 2)(4m + 2)(5m - 3)$

(f) $(2m + 2)(6m - 3)(4m - 1)$

2. Fully expand and simplify these expressions:

(a) $5(y - 1)^2$

(b) $2(y + 2)^2$

(c) $3(y + 3)^2$

(d) $3(y - 2)^3$

(e) $2(y + 1)^3$

(f) $3(y + 4)^3$

3. Write the expression for the volume of each shape. Give your answer in the simplest form. All measurements are in cm.

(a)

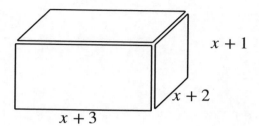

$x + 1$

$x + 2$

$x + 3$

_____

(b)

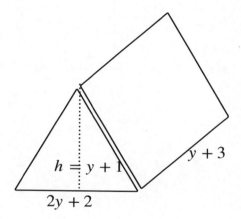

$h = y + 1$

$y + 3$

$2y + 2$

_____

(c)

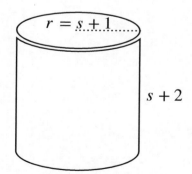

$r = s + 1$

$s + 2$

_____

6. Factorising by Common Factors

Example:

$8n + 64$

Solution:

$8n + 64$ $8n$ and 64 have common factor of 8.

$= 8(n + 8)$

Example:

$24x - 42y + 36$

Solution:

$24x - 42y + 36$ $24x$,$42y$ and 36 have common factor of 6.

$= 6(4x - 7y + 6)$

Example:

$21x^2 + 35xy$

Solution:

$21x^2 + 35xy$ $21x^2$ and $35xy$ have common factor of x.

$= 7x(3x + 5y)$

Exercise 6:

1. Fully factorise these expressions:

(b) $4k + 24$

$$\underline{4(K + 6)}$$

(b) $28y + 7$

$$\underline{7(4y + 1)}$$

(c) $26t + 39$

$$\underline{13(2t + 3)}$$

(d) $24p - 4q$

$$\underline{4(6p - q)}$$

(e) $9x - 12y$

$$\underline{3(3x - 4y)}$$

(f) $4pq + 28pr$

$$\underline{4p(q + 7r)}$$

2. Fully factorise these expressions:

(a) $6xy - 18xc + 24$

$6x\left(y - 3c + 4\right)$

(b) $13ab + 26b + 52$

$13b\left(a + 2 + 4\right)$

(c) $21pq - 15py - 9p$

$3p\left(7q - 5y - 3\right)$

(d) $14t + 28st - 7s$

$7t\left(2 + 4s - s\right)$

(e) $6df - 18ef + 15f$

$3f\left(2d - 6e + 5\right)$

(f) $25mn + 45m - 20np$

$5m\left(5n + 9 - 4p\right)$

3. Fully factorise these expressions:

(a) $24x^2y^2 + 16x^4y^3 + 8xy$

$8xy(3xy + 2x^3y^2 + 1)$

(b) $17a^2b^2 + 34a^5b^8 - 51a^3b^4$

$17ab(ab + 2a^4b^7 - 3a^2b^3)$

(c) $21m^8n^5 + 35m^2n^2 + 14mn$

$7mn(3m^7n^4 + 5mn + 2)$

(d) $48u^3v^4 - 16u^7v^6 + 32u^6v^4$

$16uv(3u^2v^3 - u^6v^5 + 2u^5v^3)$

(e) $22p^{12}q^6 - 11p^{10}q^3 + 33p^8q^3$

$11pq(2p^{11}q^5 - p^9q^2 + 3p^7q^2)$

(f) $52s^2t^2 + 26s^6t^4 - 65s^5t^3$

$13st(4st + 2s^5t^3 - 5s^4t^2)$

4. Fully factorise these expressions:

(a) $2ax^3 - 4bx^2 + 6cx$

$$2x\left(ax^2 - 2bx + 3c\right)$$

(b) $8by^4 + 2by^3 - 6y^2$

$$2y^2\left(4by^2 + by - 3\right)$$

(c) $4m^4n^2p - 2n^2p + m^2n^2p$

$$n^2p\left(4m^4 - 2 + m^2\right)p$$

(d) $10a^2b + 15b^2 - 20abc$

$$5b\left(2a^2 + 3b - 4ac\right)$$

(e) $5p^2q - 30pq + 15pq^2r$

$$5pq\left(p - 6 + 3qr\right)$$

(f) $12u^6v^2 + 30u^2v^3 - 42u^3$

$$6u^2\left(2u^4v^2 + 5v^3 - 7u\right)$$

5.Fully factorise these expressions:

(a) $(3a^2b)^3 + 9a^3b^2 - 3a^2b^4$

(b) $(-4x^3y^2)^3 - 2x^5y^2 + (2xy^2)^2$

(c) $2mn^4 + 2(m^2n^2)^3 - (4mn)^2$

(d) $4u^2v^4 - (2u^2v)^2 - (2u^3v^3)^2$

(e) $3st^2 + (3st)^3 + (3s^2t^2)^2$

(f) $10f^2g^6 - (f^2g^2)^4 - (5fg^2)^2$

7. Factorising by Grouping

Example:

$$6(a + 3)^2 - 3(a^2 - 9)$$

Solution:

$6(a + 3)(a + 3) - 3(a + 3)(a - 3)$ Factorise $a^2 - 9$ into $(a + 3)(a - 3)$.

$= 3 \times 2(a + 3)(a + 3) - 3(a + 3)(a - 3)$ 6 may be written as 3×2.

$= 3(a + 3)[2(a + 3) - (a - 3)]$ Factorise common expression $3(a + 3)$.
$= 3(a + 3)(2a + 6 - a + 3)$

$= (3a + 9)(a + 9)$

Example:

$$fg + gu - rf - ru$$

Solution:

$= g(f + u) - r(f + u)$ Group the terms with the same letters.

$= (f + u)(g - r)$

Exercise 7:

1. Fully factorise these expressions:

(a) $ef - eg + hf - hg$

(b) $ab + bc + ad + dc$

(c) $mn - mp + qn - qp$

(d) $3xz + 6zy + 9wx + 18wy$

(e) $6ab - 4b + 12ac - 8c$

(f) $8y - 16z + 7xy - 14xz$

2. Fully factorise these expressions:

(a) $xy^2 - yz^2 - xy + z^2$

(b) $3b^2 - 6bc + 2ab - 4ac$

(c) $5y^2 - 6y - 5y + 6$

(d) $4a^2 - 8a - 6a + 12$

(e) $2x^2 + 20x - 3x - 30$

(f) $12p^2 + 4pq + 15ps + 5qs$

3. Fully factorise these expressions:

(a) $14(a + 3)^2 - 7(a + 3)$

(b) $3(b - 4)^3 - 6(b - 4)^2$

(c) $2(m + 2)^2 + 3(m + 2)$

(d) $6(n + 8)^4 + 3(n + 8)^3$

(e) $12(f - 5)^2 - 2(f - 5)$

(f) $4(g - 6)^3 - 8(g - 6)^2$

4. Fully factorise these expressions:

(a) $16r^5 - 64r^4 - 32r^3 + 96r^2$

(b) $20m^4 - 40m^3 + 10m^2 - 20mn$

(c) $126p^4 - 36p^3 - 72p^2 + 18p$

(d) $63y^4 - 18y^3 + 90y^2 - 45y$

(e) $30x^3 - 12x^2 + 20x^2y - 8xy$

(f) $36ac - 18a^2 + 12bc - 6ab$

5.

(a) The area of the rectangle is $(2gf + 3f - 10g - 15)\,cm^2$.

The width of the rectangle is $(f - 5)\,cm$.

Find the length of the rectangle.

Area $= (2gf + 3f - 10g - 15)\,cm^2$ $(f - 5)\,cm$

(b) The area of the parallelogram is $(3ab + 4a - 9b - 12)\,cm^2$.

The height is $(a - 3)\,cm$.

Find the length of base.

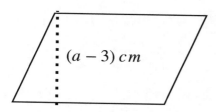

$(a - 3)\,cm$

8. Factorising Expressions of the Form $x^2 + bx + c$

Example:

$x^2 - 11x + 28$

Solution:

$x^2 - 11x + 28$ Find two numbers whose product is $+28$ and

whose sum is -11.

$= x^2 - 4x - 7x + 28$ Write $-11x$ as $-4x - 3x$.

$= x(x - 4) - 7(x - 4)$ Factorise by grouping. The bracket term must be the same.

$= (x - 4)(x - 7)$ $(x - 4)$ is a common factor.

Example:

$x^2 - 5x - 84$

Solution:

$x^2 - 5x - 84$ Find two numbers whose product is -84 and

whose sum is -5.

$= x^2 + 7x - 12x - 84$ Write $-5x$ as $+7x - 12x$.

$= x(x - 7) - 12(x - 7)$ Factorise by grouping. The bracket term must be the same.

$= (x - 7)(x - 12)$ $x - 7$ is a common factor.

Exercise 8:

1. Fully factorise these expressions:

(a) $x^2 + 9x + 20$

(b) $x^2 + 13x + 12$

(c) $x^2 + 10x + 24$

(d) $y^2 + 15y + 36$

(e) $y^2 + 23y + 132$

(f) $y^2 + 17y + 52$

2. Fully factorise these expressions:

(a) $x^2 - 7x + 12$

_____

(b) $x^2 - 13x + 40$

_____

(c) $x^2 - 12x + 35$

_____

(d) $y^2 - 15y + 50$

_____

(e) $y^2 - 16y + 48$

_____

(f) $y^2 - 20y + 51$

_____

3.Fully factorise these expressions:

(a) $a^2 + a - 30$

(b) $a^2 + 8a - 33$

(c) $a^2 - 3a - 88$

(d) $b^2 + b - 12$

(e) $b^2 + 8b - 20$

(f) $b^2 + 7b - 60$

4.The sum of two numbers is 20, and their product is 99. The two numbers are integers. What are these two numbers?

5. The area of a rectangle is $y^2 + 3y - 18$, and its is $y + 6$.

Find the width of the rectangle.

6. Karen is younger than Charlotte.

David is older than Charlotte.

Charlotte is y years old.

The product of their age is $y^3 - 3y^2 - 18y$.

Find Karen's and David's ages in terms of y.

9. Factorising Quadratic of the Form $ax^2 + bx + c$

Example:

$6x^2 + 11x + 3$

Solution:

$6x^2 + 11x + 3$ Find two numbers whose product is $+18$ and whose sum is $+11$.

$= 6x^2 + 2x + 9x + 3$ Write $+11x$ as $+2x + 9x$.

$= 2x(3x + 1) + 3(3x + 1)$ Factorise by grouping.

     The bracket term must be the same.

$= (3x + 1)(2x + 3)$ $(3x + 1)$ is a common factor.

Example:

$12y^2 - y - 6$

Solution:

$12y^2 - y - 6$ Find two numbers whose product is -72 and whose sum is -1.

$= 12y^2 - 9y + 8y - 6$ Write $-y$ as $-9y + 8y$.

$= 3y(4y - 3) + 2(4y - 3)$ Factorise by grouping.

     The bracket term must be the same.

$= (4y - 3)(3y + 2)$ $(4y - 3)$ is a common factor.

Exercise 9:

1. Fully factorise these expressions:

(a) $18x^2 + 11x + 1$

(b) $15x^2 + 26x + 6$

(c) $48x^2 + 14x + 1$

(d) $12x^2 + 23x + 5$

(e) $9x^2 + 29x + 6$

(f) $6x^2 + 28x + 30$

2. Fully factorise these expressions:

(a) $3y^2 + 23y - 8$

(b) $6y^2 - 8y - 14$

(c) $25y^2 - 15y + 2$

(d) $6y^2 + 5y - 4$

(e) $21y^2 - 6y - 15$

(f) $8y^2 + 10y - 42$

3. Fully factorise these expressions:

(a) $12m^2 - 26m + 12$

_____

(b) $34m^2 + 66m - 4$

_____

(c) $40m^2 - 75m + 35$

_____

(d) $12n^2 - 30n + 18$

_____

(e) $8n^2 - 26n + 6$

_____

(f) $18n^2 - 30n + 12$

_____

10. Factorising the Difference of Two Squares

Example:

$36x^2 - 49$

Solution:

$(6x)^2 - 7^2$ Find the positive square root of 36 and 49.

$= (6x + 7)(6x - 7)$ Apply the identity $A^2 - B^2 = (A + B)(A - B)$.

Example:

$y^2 - 121$

Solution:

$(y)^2 - (11)^2$ Find the positive square root of 121.

$= (y + 11)(y - 11)$ Apply the identity $A^2 - B^2 \equiv (A + B)(A - B)$.

Example:

$75s^2 - 48t^2$

Solution:

$= 3(25s^2 - 16t^2)$ Find the lowest common factor of 75 and 48.

$= 3[(5s)^2 - (4t)^2]$ Factorise.

$= 3(5s + 4t)(5s - 4t)$ Apply the identity $A^2 - B^2 \equiv (A + B)(A - B)$.

Exercise 10:

1. Fully factorise these expressions:

(a) $9x^2 - 4$

(b) $16x^2 - 64$

(c) $25x^2 - 49$

(d) $121x^2 - 25$

(e) $144x^2 - 36$

(f) $169x^2 - 100$

2. Fully factorise these expressions:

(a) $y^2 - 81$

(b) $y^2 - 225$

(c) $y^2 - 16$

(d) $y^2 - 9$

(e) $y^2 - 144$

(f) $y^2 - 400$

3. Fully factorise these expressions:

(a) $a^2 - \dfrac{1}{16}$

(b) $a^2 - \dfrac{1}{25}$

(c) $a^2 - \dfrac{4}{49}$

(d) $\dfrac{1}{4}a^2 - \dfrac{9}{25}$

(e) $\dfrac{1}{9}a^2 - \dfrac{16}{81}$

(f) $\dfrac{4}{25}a^2 - \dfrac{25}{64}$

4. Fully factorise these expressions:

(a) $36m^2 - (m+1)^2$

(b) $25m^2 - (m+3)^2$

(c) $49m^2 - (2m-5)^2$

(d) $9m^2 - (2m-3)^2$

(e) $(3-m)^2 - 16m^2$

(f) $(5-m)^2 - 64m^2$

5. Fully factorise these expressions:

(a) $16(p - 2)^2 - 49p^2$

(b) $4p^2 - 25(p + 1)^2$

(c) $25(p + 3)^2 - 36p^2$

(d) $9(p - 4)^2 - 64p^2$

(e) $169p^2 - 9(p + 7)^2$

(f) $121p^2 - 4(p - 5)^2$

6. Fully factorise and simplify these expressions:

(a) $2.61^2 - 3.39^2$

(b) $4.1^2 - 2.1^2$

(c) $(\sqrt{2} + 1)^2 - (\sqrt{2} - 1)^2$

(d) $(fg + ek)^2 - (fg - ek)^2$

(e) $(4\pi - r)^2 - (4\pi + r)^2$

(f) $(3\sqrt{3} + 2)^2 - (3\sqrt{3} - 2)^2$

ANSWERS

Exercise 1

1. $3(850 - a - b - c)$ 2. $6k$ 3. $\dfrac{Q}{4}$ 4. $S + T$ 5. $0.5R + 0.35Q$

Exercise 2

1. (a) $13t$ (b) $6b$ (c) $5s$ (d) $10n$ (e) $-12m + 8$ (f) $9t + 5$

2. (a) $2x + 6y$ (b) $7a + 4b$ (c) $9s - 7t$

   (d) $5p - 4q$ (e) $-2m + 6n$ (f) $18a - 8b$

3. (a) $17x^2$ (b) $13y^2$ (c) $7a^2$ (d) b^2 (e) $9n^2 - 9$ (f) $9m^2 + 4m + 2$

4. (a) $7ab$ (b) $x^2 + 3xy$ (c) $3pq - p^2$

   (d) $4f^2g^2 + 2fg$ (e) $-6t^2 + 6s^2 + 5st$ (f) $16mn + 7m^2n - g$

5. (a) $4x + 2y + 6$ (b) $6y + 18$ (c) $6a + b$ (d) $4pq + 2p + 3q + 9$

Exercise 3

1. (a) $-5p^2$ (b) $20r^2$ (c) $6q^2$ (d) $-18k^2$ (e) $33t^3$ (f) $-64a^3$

2. (a) $\dfrac{1}{2}p^2q$ (b) st (c) $-\dfrac{1}{9}a^3b$ (d) $-\dfrac{1}{3}g^3h^2$ (e) $-\dfrac{1}{5}mn^2$ (f) $4gf^2$

3. (a) a^6 (b) k^{-14} (c) $\dfrac{1}{64g^9}$ (d) $8m^6n^9$ (e) $\dfrac{1}{12s^4t^6}$ (f) $8p^{-9}q^{-6}$

4. (a) y^2 (b) b^3 (c) $2k^3$ (d) $5x^2$ (e) $2m^3n^2$ (f) $4p^4q^2$

5. (a) $\dfrac{3b^4c^3}{a}$ (b) $9m^4n^2$ (c) $\dfrac{t^2}{sp}$ (d) $2ab^2$ (e) $2m^3n^2p^3$ (f) $24a^2b^2c^2$

6. (a) $18x^2$ (b) $a^2 + 3a$ (c) $8y^2$ (d) $5p^2 + 7p + 2$

Exercise 4

1. (a) $4a + 8$ (b) $-6b + 18$ (c) $-5m + 5n$

   (d) $11x + 22y$ (e) $27p - 36q - 9$ (f) $8x^2 - 4x - 6$

2. (a) $5ab + 15a$ (b) $3pq + 6p$ (c) $4b^2 + 8bc$

   (d) $12m^2 + 30mn$ (e) $32t^2 - 24st$ (f) $8x^2 - 4xy$

3. (a) $-6ab - 18b^2$ (b) $-15ag - 10g^2$ (c) $-4ef + 6eg$

   (d) $-15x^2 + 6xy$ (e) $7x - 8$ (f) $13a + 27$

4. (a) $22a + 14$ (b) $12b + 28$ (c) $14p + 1$

   (d) $26t - 1$ (e) $3c - 23$ (f) $9m - 56$

5. (a) $-18d + 27$ (b) $6p + 41$ (c) $20p + 28$

   (d) $-2a^2 - 5b^2 + 6a - 15b$ (e) $3k^2 - 15k - 2q^2 + 4q$

   (f) $4m^2 - 36m - 3n^2 + 15n$

6. (a) $12mn$ (b) $4a^2 + 8ab$ (c) $15y^2 + 28xy$ (d) $16b^2\pi$ (e) $9m + 9n$

Exercise 5

1. (a) $m^3 + 6m^2 - m - 30$ (b) $m^3 + 5m^2 - 12m - 36$

   (c) $m^3 - 7m^2 + 14m - 8$ (d) $24m^3 + 10m^2 - 7m - 2$

   (e) $60m^3 - 46m^2 - 14m + 12$ (f) $48m^3 + 12m^2 - 30m + 6$

2. (a) $5y^2 - 10y + 5$ (b) $2y^2 + 8y + 8$

(c) $3y^2 + 18y + 27$

(d) $3y^3 - 18y^2 + 36y - 24$

(e) $2y^3 + 6y^2 + 6y + 2$

(f) $3y^3 + 36y^2 + 144y + 192$

3. (a) $x^3 + 6x^2 + 11x + 6$

(b) $y^3 + 5y^2 + 7y + 3$

(c) $\pi s^3 + 4\pi s^2 + 5\pi s + 2\pi$

Exercise 6

1. (a) $4(k + 6)$ (b) $7(4y + 1)$ (c) $13(2t + 3)$

(d) $4(6p - q)$ (e) $3(3x - 4y)$ (f) $4p(q + 7r)$

2. (a) $6(xy - 3c + 4)$ (b) $13(ab + 2b + 4)$ (c) $3p(7q - 5y - 3)$

(d) $7(2t + 4st - s)$ (e) $3f(2d - 6e + 5)$ (f) $5(5mn + 9m - 4np)$

3. (a) $8xy(3xy + 2x^3y^2 + 1)$ (b) $17a^2b^2(1 + 2a^3b^6 - 3ab^2)$

(c) $7mn(3m^7n^4 + 5mn + 2)$ (d) $16u^3v^4(3 - u^4v^2 + 2u^3)$

(e) $11p^8q^3(2p^4q^3 - p^2 + 3)$ (f) $13s^2t^2(4 + 2s^4t^2 - 5s^3t)$

4. (a) $2x(ax^2 - 2bx + 3c)$ (b) $2by^2(4y - 3)(y + 1)$

(c) $n^2p(4m^4 + m^2 - 2)$ (d) $5b(2a^2 + 3b - 4ac)$

(e) $5pq(p + 3qr - 6)$ (f) $6u^2(2u^4v^2 + 5v^3 - 7u)$

5. (a) $3a^2b^2(9a^4b + 3a - b^2)$ (b) $-2x^2y^2(32x^7y^4 + x^3 - 2y^2)$

(c) $2mn^2(n^2 + m^5n^4 - 8m)$ (d) $4u^2v^2(v^2 - u^2 - u^4v^4)$

(e) $3st^2(1 + 9s^2t + 3s^3t^2)$ (f) $5f^2g^4(2g^2 - f^6g^4 - 5)$

Exercise 7

1. (a) $(f - g)(e + h)$ (b) $(b + d)(a + c)$ (c) $(n - p)(m + q)$

(d) $3(x + 2y)(z + 3w)$ (e) $2(3a - 2)(b + 2c)$ (f) $(y - 2z)(7x + 8)$

2. (a) $(xy - z^2)(y - 1)$ (b) $(b - 2c)(3b + 2a)$ (c) $(5y - 6)(y - 1)$

(d) $2(a - 2)(2a - 3)$ (e) $(x + 10)(2x - 3)$ (f) $(3p + q)(4p + 5s)$

3. (a) $7(a + 3)(2a + 5)$ (b) $3(b - 4)^2(b - 6)$ (c) $(m + 2)(2m + 7)$

(d) $3(n + 8)^3(2n + 17)$ (e) $2(f - 5)(6f - 31)$ (f) $4(g - 6)^2(g - 8)$

4. (a) $16r^2(r^3 - 4r^2 - 2r + 6)$ (b) $10m(2m^3 - 4m^2 + m - 2n)$

(c) $18p(7p^3 - 2p^2 - 4p + 1)$ (d) $9y(7y^3 - 2y^2 + 10y - 5)$

(e) $2x(5x - 2)(3x + 2y)$ (f) $6(2c - a)(3a + b)$

5. (a) The length is $(2g + 3)$,   (b) The base is $(3b + 4)$.

Exercise 8

1. (a) $(x + 5)(x + 4)$ (b) $(x + 12)(x + 1)$ (c) $(x + 6)(x + 4)$

(d) $(y + 12)(y + 3)$ (e) $(y + 12)(y + 11)$ (f) $(y + 4)(y + 13)$

2. (a) $(x - 4)(x - 3)$ (b) $(x - 5)(x - 8)$ (c) $(x - 7)(x - 5)$

(d) $(y - 10)(y - 5)$ (e) $(y - 12)(y - 4)$ (f) $(y - 13)(y - 7)$

3. (a) $(a + 6)(a - 5)$ (b) $(a + 11)(a - 3)$ (c) $(a - 11)(a + 8)$

(d) $(b + 4)(b - 3)$ (e) $(b + 10)(b - 2)$ (f) $(b + 12)(b - 5)$

4. $x = 9$ or $x = 11$

5. $y - 3$

6. Karen $= y - 6$ years, David $= y + 3$ years

Exercise 9

1. (a) $(2x + 1)(9x + 1)$ (b) $(5x + 3)(3x + 2)$ (c) $(6x + 1)(8x - 1)$

   (d) $(3x + 5)(4x + 1)$ (e) $(x + 3)(9x + 2)$ (f) $2(x + 3)(3x + 5)$

2. (a) $(y + 8)(3y - 1)$ (b) $2(3y - 7)(y + 1)$ (c) $(5y - 3)(5y + 2)$

   (d) $(3y + 4)(2y - 1)$ (e) $3(y - 1)(7y + 5)$ (f) $2(4y - 7)(y + 3)$

3. (a) $2(3m - 2)(2m - 3)$ (b) $(3m - 4)(11m - 2)$ (c) $5(m - 1)(8m - 7)$

   (d) $6(n - 1)(2n - 3)$ (e) $2(4n - 1)(n - 3)$ (f) $6(n - 1)(3n - 2)$

Exercise 10

1. (a) $(3x + 2)(3x - 2)$ (b) $16(x - 2)(x + 2)$ (c) $(5x + 7)(5x - 7)$

   (d) $(11x + 5)(11x - 5)$ (e) $36(2x + 1)(2x - 1)$ (f) $(13x + 10)(13x - 10)$

2. (a) $(y + 9)(y - 9)$ (b) $(y + 15)(y - 15)$ (c) $(y + 3)(y - 3)$

   (d) $(y + 3)(y - 3)$ (e) $(y - 12)(y + 12)$ (f) $(y - 20)(y + 20)$

3. (a) $(a + \frac{1}{4})(a - \frac{1}{4})$ (b) $(a + \frac{1}{5})(a - \frac{1}{5})$ (c) $(a + \frac{2}{7})(a - \frac{2}{7})$

   (d) $(\frac{1}{2}a + \frac{3}{5})(\frac{1}{2}a - \frac{3}{5})$ (e) $(\frac{1}{3}a + \frac{4}{9})(\frac{1}{3}a - \frac{4}{9})$ (f) $(\frac{2}{5}a + \frac{5}{8})(\frac{2}{5}a - \frac{5}{8})$

4. (a) $(7m + 1)(5m - 1)$ (b) $(6m + 3)(4m - 3)$ (c) $(9m - 5)(5m + 5)$

   (d) $(5m - 3)(m + 3)$ (e) $3(m + 1)(3 - 5m)$ (f) $(-9m + 5)(7m + 5)$

5. (a) $(11p - 8)(-3p - 8)$ (b) $(7p + 5)(-3p - 5)$ (c) $(15 - p)(15 + 11p)$

   (d) $(-5p - 12)(11p - 12)$ (e) $(16p + 21)(10p - 21)$ (f) $(13p - 10)(9p + 10)$

6. (a) -4.68 (b) 12.4 (c) $4\sqrt{2}$

   (d) $4fgek$ (e) $-16\pi r$ (f) $24\sqrt{3}$

ALGEBRA FUNDAMENTALS

Also in this series:

Linear equations

Quadratic equations

Simultaneous equations

Printed in Great Britain
by Amazon

11 Plus Maths

Twenty Minute

Tests

CONTENTS

Introduction

This book contains 12 maths papers to begin early preparation for the 11+, SATs, or to provide a boost for any students aiming to strengthen core numeracy skills. The papers can be used as timed tests (see below) or as teaching aids.

Each paper builds on the last with questions developing in difficulty. Having completed all 12 papers, the student will be ready to move on to books at a higher level.

Although the tests are designed to last 20 minutes, children with less experience may require more time, possibly dividing each paper into two 15-minute sessions.

Papers 1 to 10

Each paper consists of a variety of questions worth 30 marks. They begin with warmup questions to sharpen basic skills, then move on to questions involving the application of knowledge and more complex thought processes.

Papers 11 and 12

Papers 11 and 12 provide a greater challenge. They offer a taste of 11+ standard questions to determine if the child is ready for more demanding material. You may wish to work through these papers with the child and discuss those extra challenges along the way.

Students going on to enter the 11+ will need to extend their numeracy skills with further practice. This might include help from home, professional tutoring and/or the use of additional texts.

Information for Students

- Not everyone can be great at maths, but whatever your level, it's good to improve. You have already taken a great first step by opening this book, so WELL DONE.

- It's okay to make mistakes, the important thing is what happens next. The best way to improve is to check your answers and discuss any errors you made with an adult.

- Perhaps ask for a separate notebook so you can copy out and re-try the more difficult questions. It might take you several attempts to get an answer right, but pat yourself on the back for being positive and not giving up. The best thing is, the more you practice, the better you get.

Self-assessment

You may find it useful to record your scores for each paper and to reflect on how you can improve. You may find that you need to:

- learn your times tables
- ask how to answer certain types of questions
- remember to check answers if there is time

Paper 1   Score out of 30 [ ]   Percentage [ ]

Things I can do to improve.

[ ]

Paper 2   Score out of 30 [ ]   Percentage [ ]

Things I can do to improve.

[ ]

Paper 3   Score out of 30 [ ]   Percentage [ ]

Things I can do to improve.

[ ]

Paper 4   Score out of 30 [ ]   Percentage [ ]

Things I can do to improve.

[ ]

Paper 5   Score out of 30 [ ]   Percentage [ ]

Things I can do to improve.

[ ]

Paper 6   Score out of 30 ☐   Percentage ☐

Things I can do to improve.

Paper 7   Score out of 30 ☐   Percentage ☐

Things I can do to improve.

Paper 8   Score out of 30 ☐   Percentage ☐

Things I can do to improve.

Paper 9   Score out of 30 ☐   Percentage ☐

Things I can do to improve.

Paper 10   Score out of 30 ☐   Percentage ☐

Things I can do to improve.

Paper 11   Score out of 30 ☐   Percentage ☐

Things I can do to improve.

Paper 12   Score out of 30 ☐   Percentage ☐

Things I can do to improve.

Progress Chart

If you wish, you can shade in the bars to plot your progress.

Don't worry if your score goes down sometimes. Every time you complete a test and look at the mark scheme, you will be learning and improving your skills.

You can calculate the percentage by multiplying your score by 10 then dividing by 3.

Example: 19 marks: 19 x 10 = 190 $\frac{190}{3}$ = 63$\frac{1}{3}$ Record 63%

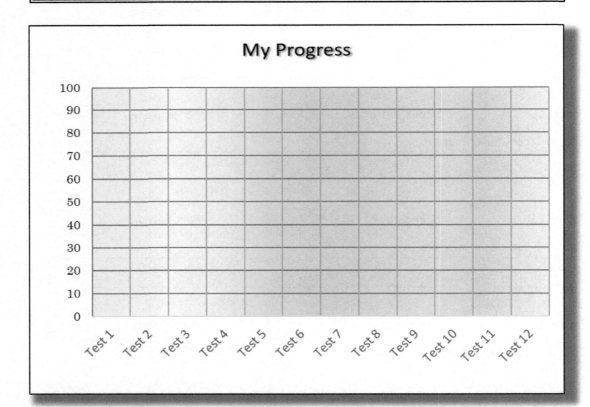

My Progress

Times Tables and Squares

1	2	3	4	5	6	7	8	9	10	11	12
2	4	6	8	10	12	14	16	18	20	22	24
3	6	9	12	15	18	21	24	27	30	33	36
4	8	12	16	20	24	28	32	36	40	44	48
5	10	15	20	25	30	35	40	45	50	55	60
6	12	18	24	30	36	42	48	54	60	66	72
7	14	21	28	35	42	49	56	63	70	77	84
8	16	24	32	40	48	56	64	72	80	88	96
9	18	27	36	45	54	63	72	81	90	99	108
10	20	30	40	50	60	70	80	90	100	110	120
11	22	33	44	55	66	77	88	99	110	121	132
12	24	36	48	60	72	84	96	108	120	132	144

13 x 13 = 169   17 x 17 = 289

14 x 14 = 196   18 x 18 = 324

15 x 15 = 225   19 x 19 = 261

16 x 16 = 256   20 x 20 = 400

3 x 3 can also be written like this: 3^2. We say three squared.

So, $3^2 = 9$, $6^2 = 36$, $10^2 = 100$ etc.

Multiplying by 10

For a whole number, just add a zero. $34 \times 10 = \mathbf{340}$

For a decimal, move the decimal place one to the right. $10.42 \times 10 = \mathbf{104.2}$

Multiplying by 5 for an even number

Example: 5×12

Divide the number by 2. $^{12}/_2 = 6$

Add a zero at the end.   **60**

Multiplying by 5 for an odd number

Example: 5×13

Take one away from the number $13 - 1 = 12$

Divide the result by 2. $^{12}/_2 = 6$

Add a five at the end.   **65**

Calculating 5% of a number

Example: 5% of 464

Shift the decimal point one place to the left   46.4

Divide this by 2.   **23.2**

(*You can find 15% by finding 5% and multiplying by 3 etc.*)

Subtract a large number from 1000

Example: $1000 - 123$

Subtract all except for the final number from 9, then subtract the final number from 10.

$9 - 1 = 8$ $9 - 2 = 7$ $10 - 3 = 7$ **877**

Will it divide?

A number is ...

Divisible by 2 if the last digit is a multiple of 2 (or is 0). So, 74 works because 4 is divisible by 2.

$^{74}/_2$ = 37

Divisible by 3 if the sum of the digits is divisible by 3. So, 72 works because the digits (7 + 2), add up to 9 which is divisible by 3.

$^{72}/_3$ = 24

Divisible by 4 if the last two digits are divisible by 4. So, 144 works because 44 is divisible by 4.

$^{144}/_4$ = 36

Divisible by 5 if the last digit is 0 or 5. So, 225 works.

$^{225}/_5$ = 45

Divisible by 9 if the sum of the digits is divisible by 9. So, 981 works since 9 + 8 + 1 = 18, which is divisible by 9.

$^{981}/_9$ = 109

Divisible by 10 if the number ends in a 0.

$^{8910}/_{10}$ = 891   (Move the decimal place one to the left: *8910.0 → 891.0*)

Paper One

1)   a) 24 + 37

.... (1)

b) 138 + 22

.... (1)

2)   a) 24 - 11

.... (1)

b) 138 - 29

.... (1)

3)   a) 8 x 12

.... (1)

b) 11 x 11

.... (1)

4)   a) 60 ÷ 15

.... (1)

b) 81 ÷ 9

.... (1)

5) How many halves go into each of these numbers?

a) 2

.... (1)

b) 5

.... (1)

6) Estimate the value 75 on this number line by drawing an arrow.

0   100

.... (1)

1

7) To find the mean, add a set of numbers together and divide by how many numbers there are.

Find the mean of the following set of numbers...

4   4   6   8   3

.... (1)

8) Place numbers in the blank squares to make the sums correct.

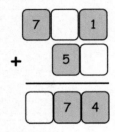

(1)

9) On a map, 12km is represented by 1cm.

The distance on the map between two towns is 7cm. How many kilometres are the towns apart?

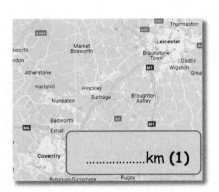

..................km (1)

1 kg = 1000 g

10) Complete these addition sums giving your answer in kg.

a) 3.9 kg add 1000 g

..................kg (1)

b) 1.6 kg add 2300 g

..................kg (1)

c) 600 g add 1200 g

..................kg (1)

11) Write down the next number in these sequences.

  a) 5   11   17   23   29

.... (1)

  b) 23   19   15   11   7

.... (1)

  c) 1   2   4   7   11

.... (1)

 d)   Write the next two numbers in this sequence.

  14   10   18   12   22   14

.... (2)

12) Write these decimals as fractions in their simplest form.

a) 0.5

.... (1)

b) 0.25

.... (1)

c) 0.6

.... (1)

13) My watch says that the time is 3.55 pm, but it is 10 mins slow. What is the real time?

.... (1)

14)

  a)   2.45 pm + 25 mins =

.... (1)

  b)   3.40 pm + 20 mins =

.... (1)

  c)   4.55 pm + 35 mins =

.... (1)

  d)   5.25 pm + 40 mins =

.... (1)

3

4

Paper Two

1)   a) 123 + 234

        .... (1)

      b) 145 + 65

        .... (1)

2)   a) 121 − 32

        .... (1)

      b) 34 - 15

        .... (1)

3)   a) 123 × 3

        .... (1)

      b) 6 × 14

        .... (1)

4)   a) 21 ÷ 5 (give your answer as a mixed number)

        .... (1)

      b) 75 ÷ 15

        .... (1)

5) What is halfway between these numbers?

   a) 24 and 42

        .... (1)

   b) 93 and 121

        .... (1)

6) Which two of the following shapes have $\frac{3}{4}$ of their area shaded?

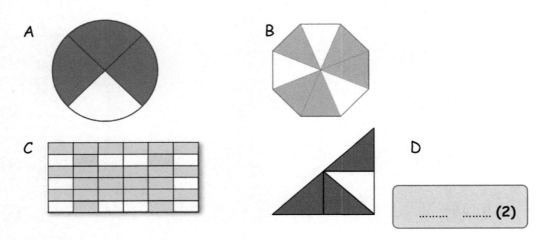

A

B

C

D

.... **(2)**

7) The pie chart shows how much money Josie spends on Christmas presents.

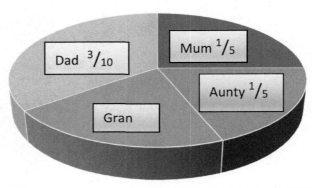

Dad $^3/_{10}$

Mum $^1/_5$

Aunty $^1/_5$

Gran

a) What fraction of her money does Josie spend on Gran?

.... **(1)**

If she has £100 altogether, how much does she spend on

b) Dad?

.... **(1)**

c) Mum?

.... **(1)**

d) Aunty + Gran?

.... **(1)**

6

8) Write the following numbers to 2 decimal places, e.g., 34.989 = 34.99

  a) 28.577

  .... (1)

  b) 1.0066

  .... (1)

9) Out of one hundred people, 75 had been to either Spain, France or both. 32 people had been to both Spain and France. 15 people had been to Spain but not France. 25 people had been to neither Spain nor France.

Complete the Venn diagram of this information to work out how many people had only been to France.

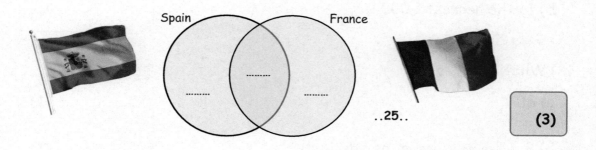

(3)

10) <u>Estimate</u> the value 33 on this number line by drawing an arrow.

0

100

(1)

7

11) a) Fay made three purchases spending £2.20, £8.20 and £3.80. How much change does she get from £20?

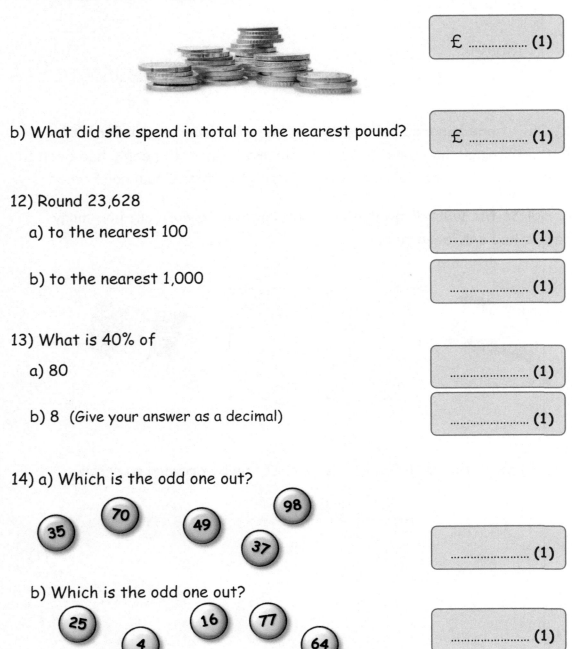

£ .... (1)

b) What did she spend in total to the nearest pound?

£ .... (1)

12) Round 23,628

a) to the nearest 100

.... (1)

b) to the nearest 1,000

.... (1)

13) What is 40% of

a) 80

.... (1)

b) 8 (Give your answer as a decimal)

.... (1)

14) a) Which is the odd one out?

35   70   49   98   37

.... (1)

b) Which is the odd one out?

25   4   16   77   64

.... (1)

Paper Three

1)   a) 56 + 44 + 32

      .... (1)

   b) 4567 + 5432

      .... (1)

2)   a) 137 - 47

      .... (1)

   b) 1211 - 320

      .... (1)

3)   a) 14 x 14

      .... (1)

   b) 15 x 15

      .... (1)

4)   a) 64 ÷ 16

      .... (1)

   b) 99 ÷ 11

      .... (1)

5) A rectangle is 6m long and 4m wide. Srijan wants to cut it into several pieces each of which measures 3m by 2m. What is the most number of pieces he can make?

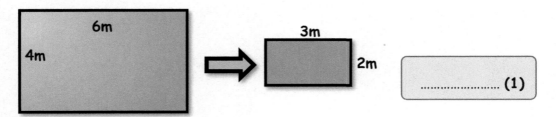

      .... (1)

6) Fill in the missing numbers in this table (the first row is done for you).

	Number	Number of quarters
	1	4
a)	12	
b)		9
c)	4.25	
d)		20

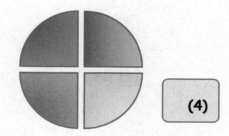

(4)

7) A circle is at coordinates (7,4) as shown.
What are the new coordinates if it moves 5 places to the left, followed by 4 places up, followed by 8 places to the right?

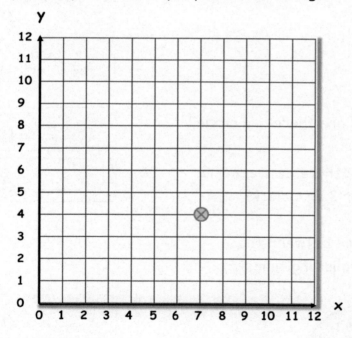

.... (1)

11

8) Place numbers in the blank squares to make the sum correct.

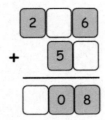

(1)

9) A quarter of a half of 40 is 5.   [$\frac{1}{2}$ x 40 = 20. $\frac{1}{4}$ x 20 = 5]

What is a quarter of a half of

    a) 16 ?

.... (1)

    b) 80 ?

.... (1)

    c) 120 ?

.... (1)

10) a) How many degrees are there in a circle?

.... (1)

b) How many degrees are there between the number 2 and the number 3 on a clock?

.... (1)

What is the smallest angle between the hands on a clock at the following times?

c) 1 pm

.... (1)

d) 3 pm

.... (1)

e) 8.00 pm

.... (1)

11) a) How many mm are there in one cm?

.... (1)

b) How many cm are there in one metre?

.... (1)

Now complete these addition sums with mm, cm. Give your answer in cm. Hint: First you need to change the mm into cm.

c) 4mm add 20cm

.................cm (1)

d) 7mm add 30.5cm

.................cm (1)

e) 5cm add 40mm

.................cm (1)

12) Jenna chooses a number. She divides her number by 5 and gets an answer of 6. What was her number?

.... (1)

13) Which number is less than a quarter of 40 and more than a third of 24?

89   9   3   17   7

.... (1)

Paper Four

1)   a) 314 + 238

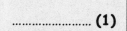 .... (1)

   b) 838 + 327

.... (1)

2)   a) 384 − 171

.... (1)

   b) 546 − 218

.... (1)

3)   a) 16 × 16

.... (1)

   b) 160 × 160

.... (1)

4)   a) 180 ÷ 90

.... (1)

   b) 180 ÷ 9

.... (1)

5) If a chocolate cookie costs 57p, how much
do three cookies cost?

£ .... (1)

6) If 4 scones cost 84p, how
much does one Scone cost?

.... p (1)

7) Write these fractions as decimals. (Hint: $\frac{18}{100}$ = 0.18)

a) $\frac{35}{50}$

.... (1)

b) $\frac{30}{150}$

.... (1)

8) a) Laura picks a number. Double the number is 36.
What is half of the number?

.... (1)

b) Jules picks a number. The number plus 7 is 13.
What is three times the number?

.... (1)

9) The internal angles of a triangle add up to 180°
a) What is the missing angle 'A' in this triangle?

51

A   38

.... (1)

b) What is the missing angle 'B' in this triangle?

B

28   42

.... (1)

10) Work out the mean for the following sets of numbers.

a) 20 40 15 45

.... (1)

b) 23 67 14 26 20

.... (1)

16

11) a) How many hours are there in a day?

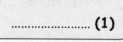

.... (1)

b) Lola the rabbit sleeps for 6 hours each day.
What fraction of Lola's life is spent awake?

.... (1)

12) 50 children filled in a survey about what they prefer to have for breakfast.

Breakfast	No. of children
Porridge	5
Cornflakes	
Pancakes	6
Wheat pops	18
Toast	2
Fruit	7

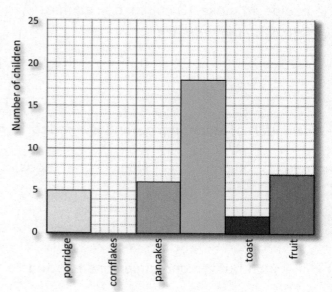

a) Fill in the missing number for Cornflakes.

(1)

b) Draw the missing bar on the chart.

(1)

c) What fraction of the children prefer porridge?

.... (1)

13) Write these numbers to 2 decimal places. E.g., 47.912 = 47.91

   a) 14.372

.... (1)

   b) 12.476

.... (1)

14) Aidan is making cupcakes.

The recipe to make 10 cupcakes requires
the following ingredients.

120g butter
230g sugar
310g flour
10 eggs

a) How much of each ingredient is needed to make one cupcake?

butter	sugar	flour	eggs
....	....	....	....

2 or 3 correct = 1 mark

(2)

b) How much butter and sugar are needed to make four cupcakes?

butter	sugar
....	....

(2)

c) On a different day, Aidan has 360g butter,
690g sugar, 930g flour and 30 eggs. How many
cupcakes can he make?

.... (1)

Paper Five

1) a) 1023 + 3298

      .... (1)

   b) 7 + 23.9

      .... (1)

2) a) 457 − 369

      .... (1)

   b) 169 - 171

      .... (1)

3) a) 230 x 30

      .... (1)

   b) 2300 x 3

      .... (1)

4) a) 360 ÷ 18

      .... (1)

   b) 90 ÷ 15

      .... (1)

5) A rectangle is 3m long and 3m wide. Sarah wants to cut it into several pieces each of which measures 2m by 1m. How many pieces can she make?

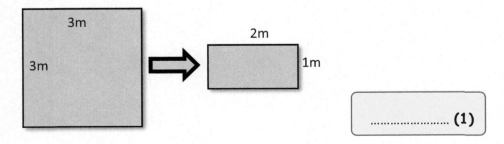

      .... (1)

6) If the digit 6 is replaced by the digit 7 in each of the numbers below, which number is increased by the largest amount?

203367   9586   862   41681

.... (1)

7) Which is the largest value in each of the pairs of numbers below?

a)   0.5   or $\frac{1}{5}$

.... (1)

b)   0.25   or $\frac{2}{5}$

.... (1)

c)   3.7   or   3.25

.... (1)

8)   a)   2.25 pm + 47 mins =

.... (1)

   b)   11.40 pm + 22 mins =

.... (1)

   c)   4.55 pm − 35 mins =

.... (1)

   d)   5.25 pm − 40 mins =

.... (1)

9) Place numbers in the blank squares to make the sum correct.

6		5

+ | 3 | |

| | 7 | 0 |

(1)

21

10) The ratio 20:5 can be written more simply as 4:1.

What is the simplest way to write the ratio 100:4?

.... : .... (1)

11) Write these numbers in order of size, starting with the smallest.

50.2 7^2 50.09 $\dfrac{100}{2}$

.... (2)

3 in the right order scores 1 mark

12)   Asdi   1 kg potatoes for £6.90

            Sunsburys   100g potatoes for 70p

            Mortisons   250g potatoes for £2.00

a) If I go to Sunsburys to buy 1kg of potatoes, how much will it cost?

.... (1)

b) If I go to Mortisons to buy 1kg of potatoes, how much will it cost?

.... (1)

c) Which shop should I buy 1kg of potatoes from to spend the least amount of money?

.... (1)

13) What is the area of this shape?

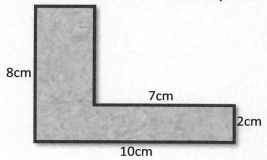

8cm

7cm

2cm

10cm

..............cm² (1)

14) The product of two numbers is 24.
They add up to 10.
What are the two numbers?

.... (2)

15) A shop checks its stock of cans of paint and records the numbers on a bar chart.

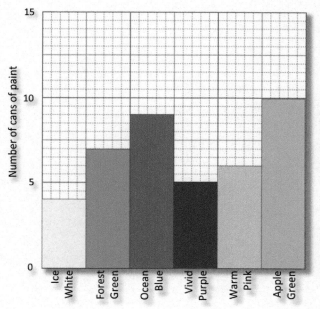

a) In which colour do they have the most cans?

.... (1)

b) How many more Apple Green cans are there than Vivid Purple?

.... (1)

c) How many more Ocean Blue cans are there than Warm Pink?

.... (1)

23

Paper Six

1)   a) 8 + 32.7   .... (1)

     b) 10.2 + 32.7   .... (1)

2)   a) 56 - 120   .... (1)

     b) 6.9 − 3.7   .... (1)

3)   a) 5.5 × 3   .... (1)

     b) 230 × 30   .... (1)

4)   a) 150 ÷ 15   .... (1)

     b) 360 ÷ 90   .... (1)

5) Put these numbers in order of size.

37% $\frac{1}{4}$ 0.23 $\frac{3}{5}$ smallest .... largest **(2)**

3 in the right order scores 1 mark

6) a) Aisha was absent from work for $\frac{1}{10}$ of her working year. What percentage of the year was she absent?   .... (1)

b) If her working year consisted of 300 days, for how many days was Aisha absent?   .... (1)

25

7) Place numbers in the blank squares to make the sum correct.

(1)

8) I face North, then I turn 90 degrees clockwise. Am I facing North, East, South or West?

.... (1)

9) What is a quarter of a tenth of 600?

.... (1)

10) Consecutive numbers are one apart, for example, 2, 3 and 4 are three consecutive numbers.

a) Find two consecutive numbers which add up to 15.

.... (1)

b) Find three consecutive numbers which add up to 24. One of the numbers is 9.

.... (1)

c) Find three consecutive which give 60 when multiplied together. One of the numbers is 4.

.... (1)

11) a) What is 48 months in years?

.... (1)

b) What is 3 days in hours?

.... (1)

c) What is 70 days in weeks?

.... (1)

26

12) Which is the odd one out?

12   18   32   66

.... (1)

13) Which of the following numbers is a factor of (divides exactly into) 36?

5   7   8   4   11

.... (1)

14) Work out the value being shown on each number line.

a)

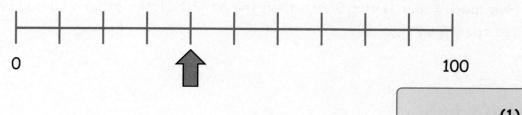

.... (1)

b)

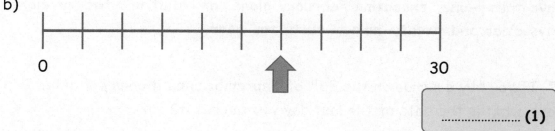

.... (1)

15) Find the mean of the following set of numbers...

7   7   8   9   4   4

.... (1)

16) The table shows the heights of three buildings.

Building	Height in metres
Shard	310
BT Tower	177
St Pauls	111

a) Add the height of the BT Tower to the height of St Pauls.

.... (1)

b) How much taller is the Shard than the height of the other two buildings added together?

.... (1)

Here is a rhyme...

Thirty days hath September, April, June and November. All the rest have thirty-one, excepting February alone, and that has twenty-eight days clear and twenty-nine in each leap year.

17) If you buy a mango on the 26th of September and it goes off after 7 days, what is the date of the last day you can eat it?

.... (1)

18) The ratio 4:8:10 can be written more simply as 2:4:5.

What is the simplest way to write the ratio 16:20:8?

...... : ...... : ...... (1)

Paper Seven

1)   a) 12 + 22.3

       .... **(1)**

       b) 8.31 + 3.27

       .... **(1)**

2)   a) 8.4 – 1.4

       .... **(1)**

       b) 4.6 – 2.4

       .... **(1)**

3)   a) 18 x 5

       .... **(1)**

       b) 121 x 5

       .... **(1)**

4)   a) 270 ÷ 9

       .... **(1)**

       b) 540 ÷ 90

       .... **(1)**

5) Consecutive odd numbers are two apart, for example, 15, 17 and 19 are three consecutive odd numbers.

a) Find three consecutive odd numbers with a sum of 21.

.... **(1)**

b) Find three consecutive odd numbers which give 105 when multiplied together.

.... **(1)**

6) Write the following numbers to 2 decimal places, e.g., 34.989 = 34.99

a) 56.772

.... (1)

b) 228.577

.... (1)

c) 49.589

.... (1)

7) Write these decimals as fractions in their simplest form.

a) 0.80

.... (1)

b) 0.45

.... (1)

8) Write these fractions as decimals.

a) three quarters

.... (1)

b) three fifths

.... (1)

9) The pie chart shows how much money Sid spends on fruit.

Apples £ 3.00   Pears £2.50   Kiwi   Grapes £2.50

a) If he spent £10 altogether, how much does she spend on Kiwi?

£ .... (1)

b) What fraction of his money does he spend on Kiwi?

.... (1)

c) What fraction of his money does Sid spend on apples?

.... (1)

10) Three numbers have a mean value of 8. Two of the numbers are 7 and 13. What is the third number?

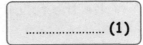 .... (1)

11) At a birthday party, 12 children said they liked cake, 11 children said they liked ice cream, and 7 of the children who liked ice cream said they also liked cake. They all liked at least one of cake and ice cream.

    a) Complete the Venn diagram.

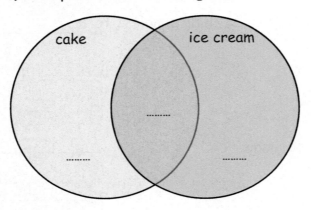

(3)

    b) How many children went to the party?

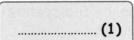 .... (1)

12) The letter y represents a number. Three times y can be written as 3y.

a) If 3y = 12, what is the value of y?

 .... (1)

Find y if ...

b) $4y = 24$

.... (1)

c) $3y + 3 = 18$

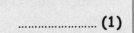 .... (1)

d) $6 + y = 21$

.... (1)

e) $4y - 10 = 30$

 .... (1)

Paper Eight

1)   a) 3.4 + 5.7   .... **(1)**

      b) 10.23 + 21.38   .... **(1)**

2)   a) $\dfrac{7}{9} - \dfrac{2}{3}$ .... **(1)**

      b) -246 + 10.5   .... **(1)**

3)   a) 2.3 × 3   .... **(1)**

      b) 23 × 0.3   .... **(1)**

4)   a) 360 ÷ 18   .... **(1)**

      b) 40 ÷ 0.80   .... **(1)**

5) Draw an arrow at the value −300 on this number line.

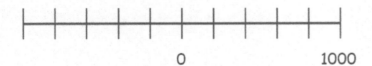

                  0   1000   .... **(1)**

6) a) Which number is **100 times greater** than six hundred and forty-three?

64030   60430   64300   6430

.... **(1)**

b) Which number is **100 times smaller** than six hundred and thirty-four?

6.34   63.40   0.634   0.60340

.... **(1)**

7) Place numbers in the blank squares to make the sum correct.

| | 4 | 1 | | 9 |
+ | 8 | 3 | 3 | 3 |

2 2 5 1 2

.... **(1)**

8) Two identical planks overlap each other by 1m. The length of the whole arrangement is 6m. Work out the length of a plank.

1m   Not drawn accurately

?

6m

.... **(1)**

9) Three numbers have a mean value of 21.
Two of the numbers are 34 and 13.
What is the third number?

.... **(1)**

10) Lizzy starts from 3 and counts up in fives.
Amar starts from 6 and counts up in threes.
What is the smallest number that both of them say?

.... **(1)**

11) Complete the magic square. Each row, column and diagonal must add up to the same number. The numbers used are 1, 2, 3, 4, 5, 6, 7, 8, 9.

One mark for each correctly completed line up to a maximum of three.

(3)

12)

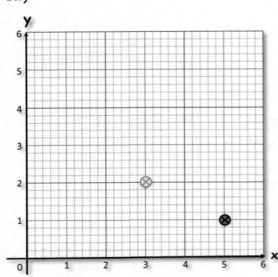

The circle at coordinates (3,2) is at the centre of a rectangle.
The circle at (5,1) is at one of the corners of the rectangle.
What are the coordinates of the other three corners?

(......,......)   (......,......)   (......,......) **(3)**

13) Write these fractions as decimals.

a) $\frac{2}{5}$

.... **(1)**

b) $\frac{4}{25}$

.... **(1)**

c) $\frac{14}{20}$

.... **(1)**

36

The common factors of 8 and 12 are 1, 2 and 4 because both 8 and 12 divide by 1, 2 and 4.

$$\frac{8}{1} = 1 \qquad \frac{12}{1} = 12 \qquad \frac{8}{2} = 4 \qquad \frac{12}{2} = 6 \qquad \frac{8}{4} = 2 \qquad \frac{12}{4} = 3$$

14) Other than 1, write the common factors of

a) 9 and 36.

.... (1)

b) 44 and 66.

.... (1)

c) 38 and 57.

.... (1)

d) 51 and 34.

.... (1)

15) Jon and Jo share 45 sweets in the ratio 4:5. How many sweets do they get each?

.... (1)

16) Lexi, Lewis and Lane share 24 grapes in the ratio 3:4:5 How many grapes do they get each?

.... (1)

Paper Nine

1)   a) 17.6 + 17.4

.... (1)

   b) $\frac{1}{6} + \frac{4}{6}$

.... (1)

2)   a) 6.44 − 8.22

.... (1)

   b) $\frac{1}{4} - \frac{1}{6}$

.... (1)

3)   a) $\frac{1}{2} \times \frac{1}{2}$

.... (1)

   b) $\frac{1}{2} \times \frac{1}{4}$

.... (1)

4)   a) 0.4 ÷ 0.8

.... (1)

   b) 40 ÷ $\frac{1}{3}$

.... (1)

5) Mo and Jai think of a number each. Mo's number is 8 more than Jai's. Their numbers multiplied together make 48.

What are the numbers?   Mo .... (1)   Jai............. (1)

6) Write these numbers in order of size, starting with the largest.

   0.22   0.023 $\frac{2}{10}$ 0.222

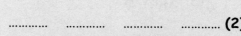

.... (2)

3 in the right order scores 1 mark

39

7) a) A rectangle is 7m long and 4m wide. Gina wants to cut it into several pieces each of which measures 3m by 2m. How many pieces can she make?

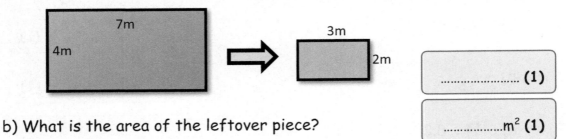

.... (1)

b) What is the area of the leftover piece?

...............m² (1)

8) Calculate the decimal equivalents of the following fractions.

a) $\dfrac{9}{12}$

.... (1)

b) $\dfrac{2}{5}$

.... (1)

c) $\dfrac{7}{20}$

.... (1)

d) $\dfrac{18}{40}$

.... (1)

9) The letter n represents a number. Find n if ...

a) $4n = 240$

.... (1)

b) $3n + 1 = 16$

.... (1)

c) $2n + 7 = 21$

.... (1)

d) $n^2 = 9$

.... (1)

10) The same type of dinner plate is sold in two different packs.

A pack of 3 is sold on Amakon for £6.25 and a pack of 12 is sold in Arkos for £24.

a) If I buy from Amakon, how much will I have to pay to get 12 plates?

.... **(1)**

b) Is it cheaper to get 12 plates from Arkos or 12 plates from Amakon?

.... **(1)**

c) What is the cheapest way to buy 18 plates and how much would it cost?

....

Cost: ....

(2)

11) a) A baby is 10 days old on February 12th.
On what day was she born?

.... **(1)**

b) Another baby is 20 days old on July 18th.
On what day was he born?

.... **(1)**

12) Dinah makes a scale model of her block of flats.
The flats are 40m tall and have a base which is 20m wide by 20m deep.
The model is 80cm tall.

a) How wide is her model?

.... **(1)**

b) What is the area in cm² of the model's base?

.... cm² **(1)**

42

Paper Ten

1)   a) $\frac{4}{5} + \frac{2}{5}$

For questions 1 and 2, give your answers as mixed numbers.

.... **(1)**

     b) $\frac{3}{7} + \frac{6}{7}$

.... **(1)**

2)   a) $2 - \frac{4}{5}$

.... **(1)**

     b) $18 - 10\frac{4}{5}$

.... **(1)**

3)   a) $\frac{1}{3} \times \frac{3}{4}$

.... **(1)**

     b) $\frac{4}{5} \times \frac{7}{8}$

.... **(1)**

4)   a) $252 \div 7$

.... **(1)**

     b) $4 \div \frac{1}{3}$

.... **(1)**

5) The volume of a cuboid (the shape below) is length x width x height.
a) What is the volume of a cuboid which is 18cm by 20cm by 5cm?

.... cm³ **(1)**

b) What is the surface area of the top of the cuboid?

.... cm² **(1)**

c) What is the total surface area of the cuboid?

.... cm² **(2)**

6) Billy went shopping and bought 3 computer games that cost £8 each and 2 doughnuts that cost £2 each.

a) How much change did Billy get from £50?

£ .... (1)

b) If the computer games had been sold with a 25% discount, how much would Billy have paid in total, including the doughnuts?

£ .... (1)

7) The difference between half of a certain number and a quarter of the number is 2. What is the number?

.... (1)

8) Find w if ...

a) $24w = 12$

.... (1)

b) $8w + 33 = 19w$

.... (1)

c) $5w - 1 = 24$

.... (1)

d) $\dfrac{w}{2} - 3 = 5$

.... (1)

9) Write these decimals as fractions in their simplest form.

a) 0.7

.... (1)

b) 0.65

.... (1)

c) 0.48

.... (1)

10) If 5 miles is the same as 8 kilometres...

a) How many miles are equal to 24 kilometres?

.... (1)

b) How many kilometres are equal to 2.5 miles?

.... (1)

c) How many kilometres are equal to 7.5 miles?

.... (1)

11) Draw an arrow at the value 10.5 on this number line.

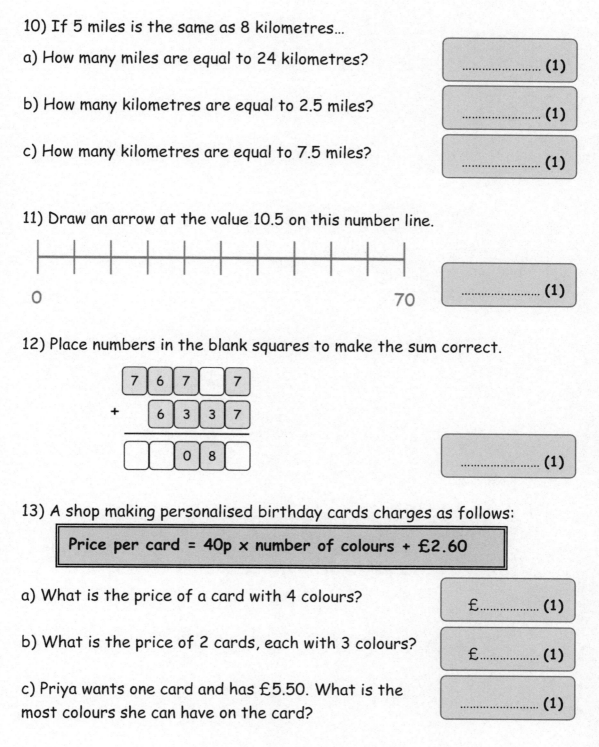

0   70

.... (1)

12) Place numbers in the blank squares to make the sum correct.

```
  7 6 7 □ 7
+   6 3 3 7
  ─────────
  □ □ 0 8 □
```

.... (1)

13) A shop making personalised birthday cards charges as follows:

Price per card = 40p x number of colours + £2.60

a) What is the price of a card with 4 colours?

£................ (1)

b) What is the price of 2 cards, each with 3 colours?

£................ (1)

c) Priya wants one card and has £5.50. What is the most colours she can have on the card?

.... (1)

45

The following two papers include some more challenging questions.

Paper Eleven

1)   a) $\frac{1}{5} + \frac{3}{10}$

         .... (1)

     b) $\frac{3}{4} + \frac{6}{8}$ (give your answer as a mixed number)

         .... (1)

2)   a) $1 - \frac{3}{5} - \frac{1}{5}$

         .... (1)

     b) $8\frac{2}{5} - 1\frac{4}{5}$ (give your answer as a mixed number)

         .... (1)

3)   a) 0.7 x 0.07

         .... (1)

     b) $\frac{1}{4}$ x $\frac{3}{4}$

         .... (1)

4)   a) $\frac{2}{3} \div 5$

         .... (1)

     b) $0.4 \div \frac{1}{3}$

         .... (1)

5) Write these numbers to 2 decimal places. Eg. 47.912 = 47.91

    a) 0.884

         .... (1)

    b) 0.0497

         .... (1)

    c) 10.00557

         .... (1)

6) George turned on a microwave oven and plotted the temperature of some milk.

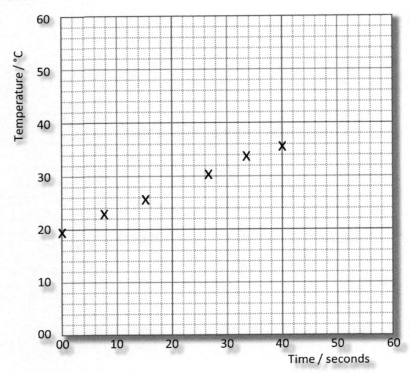

a) Draw a trend line through the points up to 40 seconds.

(1)

b) Estimate the temperature at 20 seconds?

..............°C (1)

c) Add a line on the graph to show what might happen to the temperature if the microwave switches off after 40 seconds.

(1)

7) a) Which of the following numbers is <u>not</u> a factor of 88 ?

22   2   11   6   44

.... (1)

b) Which of the following numbers is a factor of 162 ?

7   9   8   4   11

.... (1)

8) I turn 90 degrees clockwise, 180 degrees anticlockwise and finally 45 degrees clockwise. If I want to return to my original position by turning through the smallest angle possible, in which direction should I turn and what should the angle be?

Direction .... (1)

Angle .... (1)

9) Place numbers in the blank squares to make the subtraction correct.

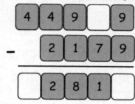

.... (1)

10) a) What is the volume of a box which is 10cm by 6cm by 4cm?

.................cm³ (1)

b) How many cubes of 2cm each side could fit into this box?

.... (1)

11)

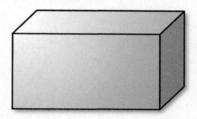

Total 73

Total 120

What is the value of each shape?

.... (1)

.... (1)

49

12) Lexi poured water from a full 400 ml jug into two identical smaller jugs, A and B, as shown on the right.

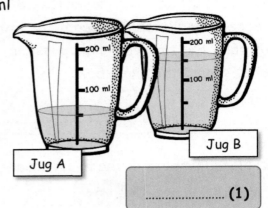

Jug A

Jug B

a) How much water was left in the 400 ml jug?

.... (1)

b) Lexi poured two-thirds of the water from jug B into glasses, then returned the rest of the water from both smaller jugs into the larger 400 ml jug. After this, how full was the larger jug?
Give your answer as a fraction.

.... (2)

13) Find m if …

    a) $8m + 33 = 19m$

.... (1)

    b) $m + 3 = 9 - m$

.... (1)

    c) $\dfrac{m}{2} + 13 = 15$

.... (1)

14) What is 338 divided by 13 ?

.... (1)

Paper Twelve

1) a) $\frac{1}{4} + \frac{3}{10}$

.... (1)

b) $\frac{1}{4} + \frac{1}{7}$

.... (1)

2) a) $\frac{3}{5} - \frac{1}{6}$

.... (1)

b) $1\frac{1}{3} - \frac{5}{6}$

.... (1)

3) a) $\frac{1}{4} \times \frac{4}{5}$

.... (1)

b) $\frac{1}{3} \times \frac{6}{7}$

.... (1)

4) a) $\frac{2}{3} \div \frac{1}{3}$

.... (1)

b) $\frac{7}{3} \div \frac{1}{6}$

.... (1)

5) What is the area of this shape?

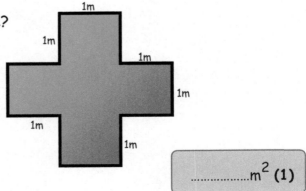

........................m^2 (1)

52

6) Complete the magic square. Each row, column and diagonal must add up to the same number. The numbers used are 2, 3, 4, 5, 6, 7, 8, 9, 10.

One mark for each correctly completed line up to a maximum of three.

(3)

7) A line joins point (2,0) to point (1,5). A second line is drawn the same length and parallel to the first, starting at point (4,1). What are the coordinates of the other end of this line? You can draw on the grid to help you.

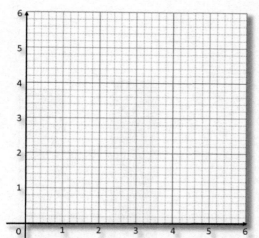

.... (1)

8) Place numbers in the blank squares to make the subtraction correct.

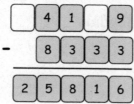

.... (1)

9) A square, ABCD, and another square, CFDE, overlap as shown.

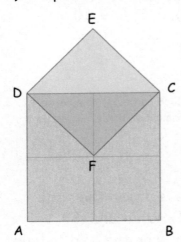

a) What is the ratio of the area of the larger square to the smaller square?

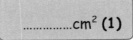
.... : .... (1)

b) What is the area of the combined shape ABCED if the distance AB is 10cm?

...............cm² (1)

10)

A shop checks its stock of rolls of fabric and records the length of each roll on a graph. For the following questions, give all answers in metres.

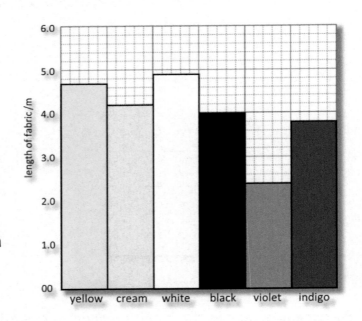

a) How much longer is the black fabric than the indigo?
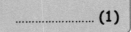
.... (1)

b) How much longer is the white fabric than the violet?
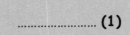
.... (1)

c) What is the average length of a roll of fabric?
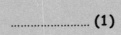
.... (1)

54

11) A small tank of water measures 10cm wide, 20cm long and 20cm deep.

If it loses 100cm³ each minute, how long does it take for the depth of the water to change by 5cm?

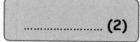

.... (2)

12)

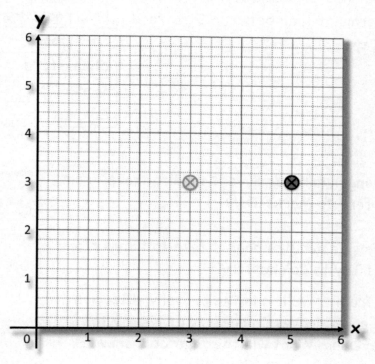

A circle at coordinates (3,3) is at the centre of a square.
A circle at (5,3) is at one of the corners of the square.
What are the coordinates of the other three corners?

(......,......) (......,......) (......,......) (3)

13) 1 coffee and 2 crème eggs costs £4.00

3 coffees and 2 crème eggs cost £8.00

What is the cost of two coffees + three crème eggs?

.... (1)

14) This is part of the timetable for trains from London Liverpool Street Station to Colchester. Chelmsford is exactly halfway in terms of time between Stratford and Marks Tey.

Liverpool Street	14.30
Stratford	14.46
Chelmsford	15.08
Marks Tey	
Colchester	15.40

a) How long in minutes does it take to travel from Stratford to Marks Tey?

.... (1)

b) How long in minutes does it take to travel from Marks Tey to Colchester?

.... (1)

c) A return train travelling in the opposite direction at the same speed leaves Colchester at twenty to nine in the evening. What will the timetable show as its arrival time in Liverpool Street?

.... (1)

15) The difference between a quarter of a certain number and one-fifth of the number is 7.
What is the number?

.... (1)

16) What is 1820 divided by 28?

.... (1)

Answers

Paper 1

1) a) 61
   b) 160
2) a) 13
   b) 109
3) a) 96
   b) 121
4) a) 4
   b) 9
5) a) 4
   b) 10
6)

7) 5
8)

9) 84km
10) a) 4.9kg
    b) 3.9kg
    c) 1.8kg
11) a) 35
    b) 3
    c) 16
    d) 26, 16
12) a) $\frac{1}{2}$
    b) $\frac{1}{4}$
    c) $\frac{3}{5}$
13) 4.05pm
14) a) 3.10pm
    b) 4.00pm
    c) 5.30pm
    d) 6.05pm

Paper 2

1) a) 357
   b) 210
2) a) 89
   b) 19
3) a) 369
   b) 84
4) a) $4\frac{1}{5}$ (4.2)
   b) 5
5) a) 33
   b) 107
6) A and D
7) a) $\frac{3}{10}$
   b) £30
   c) £20
   d) £50
8) a) 28.58
   b) 1.01
9)

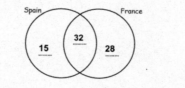

10)

11) a) £5.80
    b) £14
12) a) 23,600
    b) 24,000
13) a) 32
    b) 3.2
14) a) 37 (not a multiple of 7)
    b) 77 (not a square)

Paper 3

1)   a) 132
     b) 9,999
2)   a) 90
     b) 891
3)   a) 196
     b) 225
4)   a) 4
     b) 9
5)   4
6)   a) 48
     b) 2.25 $(2\frac{1}{4})$
     c) 17
     d) 5
7)   (10,8)
8)

9)   a) 2
     b) 10
     c) 15
10)   a) 360°
     b) 30°
     c) 30°
     d) 90°
     e) 120°
11)   a) 10
     b) 100
     c) 20.4cm
     d) 31.2cm
     e) 9cm
12)   30
13)   9

Paper 4

1)   a) 552
     b) 1,165
2)   a) 213
     b) 328
3)   a) 256
     b) 25,600
4)   a) 2
     b) 20
5)   £1.71
6)   21p
7)   a) 0.7
     b) 0.2
8)   a) 9
     b) 18
9)   a) 91°
     b) 110°
10)   a) 30
     b) 30
11)   a) 24
     b) $\frac{3}{4}$
12)   a) 12
     b) 2nd line above 10
     c) $\frac{1}{10}$
13)   a) 14.37
     b) 12.48
14)   a) 12g   23g   31g   1 egg
     b) 48g   92g
     c) 30

Paper 5

1) a) 4321
   b) 30.9
2) a) 88
   b) -2
3) a) 6,900
   b) 6,900
4) a) 20
   b) 6
5) 4
6) 41681
7) a) 0.5
   b) $\frac{2}{5}$
   c) 3.7
8) a) 3.12pm
   b) 12.02am
   c) 4.20pm
   d) 4.45pm
9)

10) 25:1
11) 7^2 $\frac{100}{2}$ 50.09   50.2
12) a) £7
    b) £8
    c) Asdi
13) 38cm^2
14) 4 and 6 (any order)
15) a) Apple green
    b) 5
    c) 3

Paper 6

1) a) 40.7
   b) 42.9
2) a) -64
   b) 3.2
3) a) 16.5
   b) 6,900
4) a) 10
   b) 4
5) 0.23 $\frac{1}{4}$ 37% $\frac{3}{5}$
6) a) 10%
   b) 30
7)

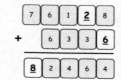

8) East
9) 15
10) a) 7,8
    b) 7, 8, 9
    c) 3, 4, 5
11) a) 4 years
    b) 72 hours
    c) 10 weeks
12) 32 (not a multiple of 3 or 6)
13) 4
14) a) 40
    b) 18
15) 6.5
16) a) 288
    b) 22
17) 3rd October
18) 4:5:2

59

Paper 7

1) a) 34.3
   b) 11.58
2) a) 7
   b) 2.2
3) a) 90
   b) 605
4) a) 30
   b) 6
5) a) 5, 7, 9
   b) 3,5,7
6) a) 56.77
   b) 228.58
   c) 49.59
7) a) $\frac{4}{5}$
   b) $\frac{9}{20}$
8) a) 0.75
   b) 0.6
9) a) £2
   b) $\frac{1}{5}$
   c) $\frac{3}{10}$
10) 4
11) a) From left to right, 5, 7, 4
    b) 16
12) a) 4
    b) 6
    c) 5
    d) 15
    e) 10

Paper 8

1) a) 9.1
   b) 31.61
2) a) $\frac{1}{9}$
   b) -235.5
3) a) 6.9
   b) 6.9
4) a) 20
   b) 50
5)
6) a) 64300
   b) 6.34
7)
8) 3.5m
9) 16
10) 18
11)
12) In any order: (1,1) (1,3) (5,3)
13) a) 0.4
    b) 0.16
    c) 0.7
14) a) 3, 9
    b) 2, 11, 22
    c) 19
    d) 17
15) 20 and 25
16) 6, 8 and 10

60

Paper 9

1) a) 35
   b) $\frac{5}{6}$
2) a) -1.78
   b) $\frac{1}{12}$
3) a) $\frac{1}{4}$
   b) $\frac{1}{8}$
4) a) 0.5
   b) 120
5) 12 and 4
6) 0.222   0.22 $\frac{2}{10}$ 0.023
7) a) 4   b) 4
8) a) 0.75   b) 0.4   c) 0.35   d) 0.45
9) a) 60
   b) 5
   c) 7
   d) 3
10) a) £25
    b) Arkos
    c) 6 from Amakon, 12 from Arkos. £36.50
11) a) Feb 2
    b) June 28
12) a) 40cm
    b) 1,600 cm^2

Paper 10

1) a) $1\frac{1}{5}$
   b) $1\frac{2}{7}$
2) a) $1\frac{1}{5}$
   b) $7\frac{1}{5}$
3) a) $\frac{1}{4}$
   b) $\frac{7}{10}$
4) a) 36
   b) 12
5) a) 1,800cm^3
   b) 360cm^2
   c) 1,100cm^2 (1 mark for 550)
6) a) £22
   b) £22
7) 8
8) a) 0.5
   b) 3
   c) 5
   d) 16
9) a) $\frac{7}{10}$
   b) $\frac{13}{20}$
   c) $\frac{12}{25}$
10) a) 15 miles
    b) 4km
    c) 12km
11)

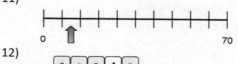

12)

13) a) £4.20
    b) £7.60
    c) 7

Paper 11

1) a) $\frac{1}{2}$
   b) $1\frac{1}{2}$
2) a) $\frac{1}{5}$
   b) $6\frac{3}{5}$
3) a) 0.049
   b) $\frac{3}{16}$ (0.188)
4) a) $\frac{2}{15}$ (0.13)
   b) 1.2
5) a) 0.88 b) 0.05 c) 10.01
6) a)

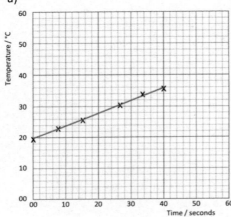

   b) $28 \pm 1°C$
   c) Line slopes down.
7) a) 6 b) 9
8) clockwise, 45 degrees

   9)

10) a) 240cm³ b) 30
11) a) 40 b) 11
12) a) 200 ml b) $\frac{3}{4}$
13) a) 3 b) 3 c) 4
14) 26

Paper 12

1) a) $\frac{11}{20}$
   b) $\frac{11}{28}$
2) a) $\frac{13}{30}$
   b) $\frac{1}{2}$
3) a) $\frac{1}{5}$
   b) $\frac{2}{7}$
4) a) 2
   b) 14
5) 5
6)

5	**10**	**3**
4	6	8
9	**2**	**7**

7) (3,6)
8)

3	4	1	**4**	9
	8	3	3	3
2	5	8	1	6

9) a) 2:1
   The overlapping section is half of the small square but a quarter of the large square, so the large square must be twice the area.
   b) 125 cm²
   The large square has an area of 100cm², so the small square is 50cm³. The total area is the large square + half of the small square. 100 + 25.
10) a) 0.2cm b) 2.5cm c) 4cm
11) 10 minutes
12) In any order: (3,1) (3,5) (1,3)
13) £7.00
14) a) 44 minutes b) 10 minutes c) 9.50 pm
15) 140
16) 65

Printed in Great Britain
by Amazon